My Handsome Boy

Susan Watkins

DEDICATION

To my three surviving children – Gareth, Stephen and Michelle, whose love and support over the years, has helped to keep Kevin's memory alive.

To my husband Rob, who, despite not being Kevin's father, has, over the past 21 years, cared and encouraged me to complete this project. He felt my story should be told, as after reading it, he began to understand my pain and grief.

CONTENTS

PROLOGUE

As I held my new born son in my arms, I stroked his face, touched his lips, kissed his forehead and cried so much that my tears made his little face wet.

I thought if I cried long and hard enough, he would open his eyes and recognise me as his mum. He had a beautiful face that reminded me of my dad, and I dearly wanted to hold his hand and see his little body, which was swaddled in green theatre sheets.

But as I started to unwrap my precious little bundle, I was stopped by the midwife. She told me it was best that I didn't see him, and that was the last time I did.

I must have dozed off to sleep with him in my arms, but when I woke up, my baby was gone.

I had really wanted to see him. I wanted to understand why my baby had died. He had looked so normal, but the green sheets had masked deformities that, had he been born today, might have briefly survived.

At that time, we weren't officially allowed to name our little boy as his had been a stillbirth, but we wanted to call him Kevin. A few weeks later, I looked up the meaning of the name, which was 'handsome'. He was indeed handsome, and now, as it has been 40 years since his birth, I'm sure he would be handsome still.

1
MY DEAR FAMILY

1982 had started like any other year. No one could have foreseen the unhappiness that would unfold as the year drew on. If I could banish any time from my life, 1982 would disappear, the pain caused by my memories is sometimes too much to bear.

I was born in January 1958, the younger of two daughters. We were a "three-generation" family then, as my fathers parents lived with us. I had a happy childhood growing up in the 1960's, but the dramatic world events of that decade made a real impression on me: the assassination of President Kennedy in Dallas and, in particular, the Aberfan disaster; which happened not far from where we lived. I was the same age as most of the children who died, and I remember my mother and grandmother weeping. It was also the decade of Woodstock, flower power and mini-skirts. I have lots of lovely memories of that time and look back with fondness of our family holidays to Devon, Burnham-on-Sea and Porthcawl.

In those days many young girls wanted to get married and have a family, and I was no exception. I liked the thought of nursing but didn't think I had the academic ability to pursue this, so I left school at 16, after my 'O' levels and CSE exams. I completed a secretarial course at a local college and worked in numerous offices. It was in one of these jobs that I met the man who was to become my first husband and father to all four of my children. I was very much in love and we got married very quickly. We bought our first house and settled into married life, and Gareth was born just over 3 years later. Within a few months of his birth, we moved to a small community a few miles outside my home town of Newport. That was when my life started to change.

We were like any other normal family, or so I thought. In the summer of 1981, we moved to a lovely new home; we had a beautiful baby son, and everything should have been perfect. But I soon found living outside Newport was a very lonely experience. My main problem was that I couldn't drive, so I felt stranded and alone. I knew no one in the town and although my new neighbours were very welcoming, I missed my family and I missed the company of my friends. My husband was ok as he was going back and forth to work, but every day I just saw the four walls of the living room.

On my birthday that January it started to snow; it was the heaviest snow I had seen since 1964 when I was a small child. It began snowing on the Thursday evening and didn't stop for two days. We were literally cut off from everywhere. The snow was at least 2 feet deep, with drifts of up to 10 feet in places. What made matters worse was, that the one supermarket in the town was stripped bare of goods, because people were panic buying. The snow virtually disappeared within 2 weeks, but by then we'd had enough and wanted to move back to Newport. We knew we would lose money, but I was desperately unhappy.

We were amazed at how quickly we sold the house, but it took ages to find one we liked back home. When we did, we first felt that it was a bit too close to my parents, but when things started to go wrong, it meant so much having help nearby. The only hitch in the move was that the young couple who were buying our house tried to stall their completion date until August, but as I had discovered I was pregnant with my second child in April, I wanted to move before I became too "bulky".

We eventually moved in June, and not only did I have to contend with a difficult pregnancy, but we were all becoming increasingly concerned about my dad's health. He had always been strong and easy going, but he was slowly becoming very emotional and experiencing mood swings and forgetfulness. We knew that he was concerned for my sister, as we all were. She was living with her family in Canada and experiencing a traumatic domestic situation. A divorce was proceeding, but we as a family could only give support via the telephone. To make matters worse, a very close family friend died suddenly in May, and Dad found the loss extremely difficult to cope with. Dad had always been the one we could lean on, but this time it was Mum who became the supporter.

Dads health progressively became much worse as the year drew on. In the autumn, we were all shocked when he was diagnosed with pre-senile dementia, aged just 55. At first, he was able to carry on working, but eventually he applied for early retirement on the grounds of ill health.

He was fortunate in that a voluntary redundancy scheme was in place at the steelworks where he was employed in order to cut down on the workforce without making any forced redundancies, and so he was notified on November the 4th that year, (the day after Kevin was born) that he would be finishing work the following day.

Having two emotional experiences within a few days caused his condition to deteriorate very rapidly, and sadly he never recovered. My mother always told people that he was never the same after Kevin died, but she had no idea how much this hurt me and I couldn't tell her as she would have been so distressed that she had upset me.

2
A MOTHER'S INSTINCT

My story about Kevin begins in June 1982, when I was 22 weeks pregnant. We had just moved back to my hometown of Newport, South Wales, and I was already mum to a 16 month old son, Gareth.

When I was carrying Gareth, I experienced quite a lot of morning sickness, but this time it was far worse. In fact, I had started vomiting three weeks before I discovered I was pregnant. The sickness became so bad that I resorted to taking medication, and although I felt weak and tired, I didn't lose any weight. I knew something was not right. Even though I'd been sick a lot during my first pregnancy, I always felt well in between bouts.

As I had a normal delivery with my first son, I was booked into the GP unit at my local hospital, where the care was shared between our own GP and the midwives at the hospital. This was a relaxed way of doing things and was much friendlier and less clinical. After all, I was only having a baby; I didn't have a serious illness.

When I was 16 weeks pregnant, I had a check-up at the hospital and blood tests were taken to check my haemoglobin (iron) levels . At the same time, I asked if an AFP (alpha-fetoprotein test) would be included, and if not, I wanted one to be carried out.

But the midwife taking my blood sample looked quite disgusted, as if I had no right to make such a request. "What makes you think you need such a test?" she said. "You've had one healthy child, haven't you? Don't be so stupid!" I was afraid to push the matter any further, but deep down I just knew something was wrong. However, I told myself it was all in my imagination and tried to put my fears behind me.

By mid-September, the sickness was easing off, but I still felt unwell. At 35 weeks, I had to be seen by either a Consultant or Senior

Registrar to ensure there would be no problems at the birth. A few days before my appointment, I experienced a four hour episode of painful discomfort and a tightening sensation similar to contractions, but I knew it was not labour. A friend of mine, who was a midwife, reassured me and told me to mention this experience when I attended the clinic.

I saw a Senior Registrar, who was very nice and reminded me more of a tailor than a doctor as he wore a tape measure around his neck! He checked me over, then disappeared for a few minutes; when he came back he told me he'd arranged a quick scan as he thought the baby was lying in the breech position (bottom first). He reassured me that the baby would probably turn, but he wanted to check the position. I told him about the experience that I'd had a few days earlier, he said it could have been the baby turning around. He took me into a small scanning room; The procedure didn't take long, but he confirmed the baby was breech. He explained that I would be transferred to the care of the consultants, but if the baby turned I could go back under the care of my GP.

I was very frightened when I got home; I didn't know what to think, and my instincts about the baby prayed on my mind. The professionals told me not to worry, but their advice just wasn't sinking in. A few days after this appointment I started experiencing terrible pains. They went on for so long that I thought I must be in labour even though there was no pattern to them. I phoned the hospital for advice and was told to go in to be assessed. I appeared to be having contractions of some sort, but I didn't seem to be in labour. I stayed in for just a few days for them to keep an eye on me. But when this happened again, I really started to worry.

I was given an appointment for a scan and X-ray on the 29th of October, just two days before the baby was due. My husband was working so I went alone. The X-ray was first. I laughed when the radiographer told me to lie on my stomach, I thought "you must be joking?", but he wasn't! He said "it's the only way to keep the little bu****rs still for the X-ray!". It was then I realised hey were X-raying the baby. It was a very strange experience watching the screen for the scan and when they measured baby's head at 10.3 centimetres, I commented that it must be a big baby. Then my view was blocked by the radiographer. The whole experience was so uncomfortable and painful that I cried buckets when I got home, and that night I was in so much pain that I was taken back into hospital.

The following day I saw the Registrar, who told me that as I was due the following day (Sunday), I should stay in, as breech deliveries are often very quick and anyway the Consultant wanted to see me on the Monday. I remember telling him that I didn't care what they did, as long as this time I took my baby home with me. He didn't say anything, but both he and the sister midwife, who was also present, just looked at each other and walked out.

3
HEART BREAKING NEWS

I spent the weekend in hospital, thinking about their reaction. On Monday morning, the Consultant told me that he wanted to see my husband as well as me, so I arranged for him to come in that afternoon. The consultant was on time, and when he came in he turned and shut the door - something he'd never done before. At that moment I knew there was something wrong with the baby.

He told us that our baby had been found to have Hydrocephalus, (put simply, water on the brain) and that was why he had turned breech, as his head was too big to move down the birth canal. If he lived, it would be for no more than five or 10 minutes after the birth. As he delivered the devastating news, my husband and I sat in silence, my hands held so tightly in his that he had marks where my nails had dug in. The Consultant offered us the option of going home to come to terms with the situation and to come in again in one or two weeks' time to be induced.

I declined the offer and went home for the night, arranging to return by 9:00 AM the following morning. After the consultant had left, and before my husband had come to take me home, the Registrar called in to see me. He apologised for not telling me on Saturday, but he explained that he wasn't permitted to comment, as it was the Consultants job to do that. He told me how sorry he was and that he would help me as much as he could. I have always found doctors to be quite distant, but he proved they are human; some just don't know how to show it. He let me cry on his shoulder - something I shall never forget.

It was very difficult telling our parents. We had a family conference, and I relayed the awful news. My father went to pieces and was very upset for many days after. My mother was very strong for me, but my husband's parents didn't really say much; I think that they were too shocked. But how were we going to deliver such heart breaking news to my 20 month old son; still a baby himself? All he knew was that he was going to have a brother or sister, so we knew explaining it to him would be very difficult. Our friends were very supportive; They had taken care of our son, while my husband and I told the family. It must have been very hard for them to do this as they were also expecting their own baby in just a few months' time.

That afternoon, after the consultant had spoken to us, my husband briefly returned to work to tell his employers that he had to go home, and didn't know when he would be back. No one questioned him; They were aware we had to see the consultant and they knew about my condition.

4
THE WORST DAY OF MY LIFE

After a very restless night, we were both up early. My son Gareth was taken to my mother's and my husband took me back to the hospital, where I was put in a single room that had been reserved for me. I asked to have a Caesarean section but my request was refused because it would leave a scar! Ironically, I would have loved that scar, as a visible reminder of my precious son's brief life.

The doctor began the induction process at 10:00 AM and I had to have an hour's bed rest. Then all we could do was wait. That day, Tuesday November the 2nd 1982, was to be one of the longest days of my life, and certainly the most agonising. My husband stayed with me all the time and even ate my lunch, as I wasn't allowed any. By 8:00 PM, my contractions were becoming stronger so I was taken to the labour ward to be assessed. But I knew that I'd been taken into the WRONG room. I had been told I'd be in a room set aside for breech and multiple births and was equipped for emergencies.

The young midwife who came in was unhelpful to the point of negligence. She didn't even look at my notes but told me I wasn't in labour as the baby's head was still positioned higher. I told her the baby was breech, but she responded by saying she knew what she was talking about and that my baby was not breech. When I asked her if she had looked at my notes, she said 'no' and in any case, she had a more important patient to see to, as she had to prepare her for a Caesarean, with that she left us but I was still contracting and in terrible pain.

At 9:00 PM, two midwives and an Auxiliary nurse with a wheelchair arrived, apologising for the mix up with the rooms. "We will get you over there now and make you comfortable" they said. They were so kind and supportive. After they had assessed me and given me pethidine, they sent me back to the ward to get some sleep, sending my husband home with an assurance that they would phone him if necessary.

I slept until 4:00 AM, by which time the contractions were very strong and very painful. I buzzed for the midwife, who arrived swiftly with a wheelchair, telling me she had been waiting for me to call. Another midwife telephoned my husband while I was taken to the labour ward, it didn't take him long to arrive.

My memories of the next few hours are vague, as I was being given pain relieving drugs intravenously and I'd inhaled large quantities of gas and air. My husband looked lost and bewildered as the staff bustled about; it was a very busy night but not once was I left alone. The staff were so caring and kind, and in fact, the sister midwife who was looking after me stayed until the doctor sent her home at around 8:45 AM. She was exhausted and had to drive some distance to get home but she stayed because she wanted to see me through it.

It was about 8:00 AM that the registrar asked my permission to put me to sleep to deliver the baby, but I refused as I wanted to do it all myself. I was tired, but I wanted to carry on, so he said he would give me a little longer. I was slowly becoming quite distant and not always aware of everything happening around me, and at 9:00 AM the registrar returned and told me I had been through enough. He said he was going to put me to sleep, as they did not want to run the risk of losing me too as I appeared to be giving up!

I started to panic, suddenly there were lots of people in the room in green theatre suits and masks. The anaesthetist introduced himself; there were people wandering around behind me, and as I couldn't see them I panicked even more. I can remember clutching the mask attached to the gas and air tank and refusing to let go. At about 9:30 AM, the anaesthetist tried to put a mask over my face but I lost all control and started crying telling them to leave me alone. I fought them off with my hands and arms: I was so frightened. After a few minutes they left me to calm down. The Anaesthetist told me that the gas and air tank was empty so he gave me a mask which was attached to a new tank, or so I thought. It was actually the mask that was attached to the oxygen that he tried to use a few minutes earlier. When my next contraction started, I put the mask to my face and he held it there, everything went black.

The next thing I knew, my husband was standing next to me holding my hand, tears cascading down his face. With trepidation, I moved my hand down to my abdomen and found it flat; my bump had gone. It was now 10:30 AM. I could only whisper to my husband "what is it?" "A little boy" he said. Then came the question I dreaded asking. "Is he dead?" My husband simply responded "Yes ".

I can remember starting to cry and asking to see my baby. I was very sleepy. Throughout the whole ordeal I would be awake for a few minutes, then I would fall asleep again. After a while, I heard the midwife say here he is, so I opened my eyes to see a clear Perspex cot with what looked like a doll inside. He was wrapped tightly in green theatre sheets, with a white sheet wrapped around his head like a turban. As soon as I saw his face, I told my husband that he looked just like my dad, but my husband said he looked like Gareth.

The midwife placed him in my arms and I looked at him, I stroked his face, touched his lips, kissed his forehead and cried. I could not believe there was anything wrong with him; He had a beautiful face. I said he looked normal, but the midwife and my husband shouted me down, repeatedly saying he was not normal. I cried again; so much that my tears made his little face wet. I thought if I cried long enough and hard enough, he would open his eyes and look at me, see me as his mum. But of course, that didn't happen. I wanted to hold his hand; Wanted to see his deformities, so I started to unwrap him. The midwife stopped me, telling me it was for the best not to see but I wanted to see; I wanted to understand!

I must have dozed off to sleep again. When I woke up, my baby was gone. I never saw him again. The midwife apologised for taking him away but she felt she would not be able to get him off me, and he had to go somewhere cool. Although we were officially not entitled to give him a name, we wanted to, so we called him Kevin. Ironically a few weeks later when I looked up the meaning of the name it meant handsome birth, and he was a handsome baby.

During the delivery, my husband had been given the option of staying with me even though I was asleep but, he decided to wait outside. The midwife felt she couldn't take him to the waiting room with the other expectant fathers, so she took him to the staff room.

The birth had been difficult, as Kevin's head was so enlarged by fluid which had to be drained off. My husband told me he heard a baby scream at about the time they said he was delivered, but the doctor said he did not live. Not only did Kevin have Hydrocephalus, but he also had a Spina Bifida lesion at the top of his back. Apparently, this is unusual as they are most commonly at the base of the spine. We didn't know about this until after the birth. Many years later I asked to see my medical notes from that time, as I still needed to understand. A colleague came with me to help decipher the jargon. He was delivered by a forceps delivery and an episiotomy. I even found out his weight, 5lb 12oz.

5
JUST ONE OF THOSE THINGS

The next few days were a blur.

Once I was ready to leave the labour ward I was taken to the gynaecological ward, where women were having miscarriages and abortions. The doctors felt it would be it would be kinder to send me there, and I was put in a room on my own at the far end of the ward. The nurses did their best, but I don't think they quite knew what to do with me.

My husband had the difficult task of having to break the news to the family. As I mentioned in a previous chapter, just a few months earlier, my dad (once such a strong character), had been diagnosed with what was then known as pre senile dementia, aged just 55; and I knew he'd be greatly distressed as the illness had made him very emotional. When he and my mother visited me that evening, he cried and hugged me, while my mother was the one who had to stay strong. But my husband said that the worst call he had to make was to my sister, 5000 miles away in Canada, and as I mentioned previously, she was having problems of her own, and took the news badly.

The next few days remain quite distorted in my mind; I felt I was outside my body watching what was happening, but I was powerless, I had no control. My bed was near the staircase and I thought I could hear the babies crying in the Post-Natal ward two floors below; my mind was working overtime and I was suffering from terrible after pains. Despite being given medication, I had an unsettled night. The next morning I declined the offer of breakfast in my room and, still groggy, made my way to the dayroom. After all I was going to have to face people sometime; there is no point in hiding away.

One of the ladies at my table noticed I had a dressing on my hand from the IVI, and asked if I'd been to theatre overnight. I hesitated, but then told her that I'd had a baby the previous morning, but he had died. She asked if I meant I had a miscarriage, but I told her I had a little boy and he died. They were very kind and sympathetic but admitted they didn't know what to say. Then I felt faint and the nurses took me back to my room, where the midwife carried out a Post-Natal check. My husband was allowed in, even though it was outside visiting hours, and the obstetric consultant came to see me. I had questions for him but he didn't have many answers for me.

After Kevin was born the consultant suggested I'd be discharged, and go home the following day, which made me feel like I was an embarrassment because my baby had died and they wanted me out of the hospital. Although I still felt unwell, I decided to go home as I desperately wanted to see Gareth. But before I left, I asked the Consultant if this would happen again. He told us it was a fluke and wouldn't happen again, then literally patted me on the head saying: "Never mind dear, go home and try again". I also asked why I had been refused an AFP blood test, as this could have detected an abnormality. His response was, the lesion was closed, so no spinal fluid had leaked and therefore the blood test wouldn't have picked anything up anyway. But I know it would have been picked up on a scan. I was appalled by the bureaucracy and patronising attitude towards me. It may have been all in a day's work to them, but my life had changed forever and nothing would ever be the same again. Six weeks after we lost Kevin, I had to see the Consultant again for my Post-Natal check-up, and to talk about what happened. He was very matter of fact about it all, telling me it was 'just one of those things' that wouldn't happen again. I had been told there may be a photograph of Kevin so I asked him about it? His reaction was simply to shrug his shoulders before looking through my medical notes. He found an envelope with my name on it which he tossed casually and unceremoniously across the desk to where we were sitting. Inside was a blurry Polaroid photograph, taken on an instant camera. But it was a photo of Kevin, my only tangible memory of him, and it became my most treasured possession. I took it home and placed it in a small bag with all the cards and letters I'd received. In later years I bought a pretty tin to keep all the letters and cards safe.

6
DENIED A FUNERAL

In the hope that something good could come out of my ordeal and that Kevin's loss wouldn't be in vain, I offered his little body for medical research. But the consultant refused and said it wasn't needed. Then I asked about burial, and was told the hospital would deal with that. We were denied a funeral because he didn't live, and I was told I couldn't see him again as he needed to be somewhere cold.

Having been denied the opportunity to arrange a funeral, I decided to write to the hospital to ask where Kevin had been buried. This preyed on my mind, as a couple of months before Kevin was born, there was a front page article in the local evening paper about the remains of a stillborn baby being found in the bushes of the cemetery, by some children playing. I was horrified at the story and felt so sorry for the parents but little did I know how closely I would relate to this later that year. I had a very nice letter back from the hospital, sending condolences and telling me that Kevin was buried in a lawned section at the rear of the cemetery and advising that if I contacted the cemetery Superintendent, I'd be able to see where my precious son was buried. I was also reassured that the people responsible for that sad incident were no longer working at the cemetery.

So, my husband and I decided to visit the grave just before Christmas that year, taking flowers with us. Sadly, the picture of the place that had been painted for us was nowhere near reality. It was just a muddy mess, with all the new graves dedicated to older people who, unlike Kevin had lived a long life. I thought there would be a separate area for babies, but there wasn't and I was distressed to see that there was no mark on Kevin's grave at all. We asked permission to put a small memorial plaque on his grave, which the cemetery superintendent agreed to. The following summer we installed a simple plaque, just bearing his first name with 'stillborn' in brackets and the date of his birth. Over the next few years, another plaque and a cross appeared with similar dates to Kevin, so it was comforting to know he wasn't alone. I started making regular visits to the cemetery, sometimes taking Gareth with me. Visiting Kevin's grave made me feel better; I couldn't do anything else for him but at least I could take him flowers.

7

FEELING SO ALONE

When I got home, I had lots of cuddles from Gareth. He wasn't yet two years old, so we hadn't told him much about where I'd been, he hadn't mentioned the baby, so we kept quiet. Later that afternoon, I was visited by a community midwife, who said that as I had been discharged so early, she just needed to check me post-Nataly.

The following morning my community midwife called. She was so lovely, caring and compassionate, telling me she was there for me if I needed her, and she would call in every day. She asked me if my GP had been in touch, I told her that he hadn't, she then asked to use the phone and called the GP. Apparently the hospital had failed in their duty of care to me, as they had not contacted my GP to tell them about my stillbirth. My GP visited after he had finished morning surgery. He too was very kind, expressing his concern and his sorrow at the news. He asked me if I needed anything to help me sleep? But I said I'd rather try to manage without. I did have some pain relief for the after pains, and also medication to dry up my milk supply, which was causing me a lot of discomfort.

Over the next few days my husband told the rest of the family, friends and neighbours, and one evening, by now feeling a little better physically, I decided I needed some fresh air, so I took a walk down to my local shop to pick up a newspaper. I was almost at the shop, when I bumped into a lady who lived a few doors down. She greeted me with a smile and said "Oh you've had your baby, what did you have?" I felt terrible for her, she obviously hadn't heard. I held her hand and told her that I had had a little boy, but he had died. There was a look of horror on her face, and she fell to her knees. I helped her up; she was apologising that she didn't know and she was so sorry. I was so shocked and distressed when I

16

got home and thought, I couldn't face that happening again. My husband and I decided to put an announcement in the local paper. It was difficult at first, because the paper didn't know which column to put the announcement in, but after some deliberation it was decided to put it in the birth column, stating he was still born.

Over the next few weeks, my community midwife visited me regularly, and continued to visit beyond the statutory 28 days, when the health visitor takes over. However, after about six weeks, she had to tell me she could no longer visit, which I could understand, but it was what she told me next that really upset me. My health visitor was not going to call on me as the baby had not survived, and she felt she was not needed. That was probably the first time I felt very alone. I was so upset.

During those first few weeks, it is difficult to explain how I felt. Gareth was a treasure and kept me going through the waking hours. But when he was asleep I began to feel miserable and very sorry for myself. The first few days were the worst and I cried constantly. I didn't think my son would notice me crying, but one day he climbed up on the settee next to me, handed me a paper tissue and said: "no crying, no more mammy", it was at that point I realised I had to pull myself together, if not for myself then for my son. I still haven't told him about his brother as he hadn't asked, but about two weeks later, I was getting him dressed one morning and he prodded my belly and asked: "Where's the baba?" my heart sank, as I had no idea what I was going to say. I managed to distract him, so I got away with it for the time being, but I needed some help.

I had grown up within the Baptist Church and had a lot of support from members, one of whom had experienced a stillbirth herself and was very supportive. I asked her for advice on what to say to my son, and she told me that as he had listened to Bible stories about Jesus when he was in the church creche, to use his name to explain where Kevin had gone. So the next time my son asked me about the baby, I explained that the baby had been very sick, and Jesus had taken him to live with him in heaven, so he wouldn't be sick anymore. He accepted this explanation and never asked again.

I felt it was important to try and get on with family life, especially for Gareth's sake, but it was very difficult for my husband and me, as he had shut himself off from his emotions, I needed to talk about Kevin, but he wouldn't let me; I know he had his own grief and guilt to deal with but I felt that I was grieving alone. I was also finding that some peoples attitude toward me had changed, or perhaps this was just how I felt in my delicate mental state. People would cross the road or turn back on themselves so they didn't have to talk to me, which made me feel very isolated. One pregnant woman even refused to stand next to me, in case what had happened to Kevin was catching. I understand that they may not have known what to say, but it didn't help me. I didn't want them to feel sorry for me, but a simple 'hello', would have been nice. If they felt uncomfortable talking about what happened, that was fine, but I wish they hadn't just ignored me.

Some evenings I just wanted to talk, especially if my husband was working. Any person to answer their phone to me was stuck with me! Most were lovely and sympathetic, but I had one experience when a 'friend', stopped me, mid-sentence, and responded with a statement! 'you are not still going on about that baby are you? He is dead for gods sake!'. I just wasn't prepared for that!

Why do some family members have to apportion blame? A hurtful comment from a sister-in-law was that Kevin's condition couldn't possibly have been inherited from their side of the family!

My paranoia and distress also prevented a disaster. The house was being rewired and all the roses in the lights had been replaced. When my husband was on nights and Gareth was asleep, I had most of the lights on, as at that time I hated being in the dark when alone. Over a few weeks a very "fishy" smell was developing, but only on my husbands night shifts. One night the smell was very strong and I felt as though the scent had drifted past me on the stairs! I was terrified; I imagined it was Kevin, come back to haunt me. I was hysterical! My husband had to come home and sit with me until I fell asleep. The following day my husband contacted the local councils environmental health department and asked them to investigate the smell.

An inspector came to the house, stood in the hallway and noticed the new plaster where the new wiring had been placed. He asked if the house had been rewired recently, which I confirmed. He asked to look at the light in the hall. He took the bulb out and unscrewed the rose fitting, he had a sniff then offered it to me to sniff and asked if that was the smell, to which I replied "yes, that's it". He asked if the smell was in every room when the lights were on, which again I confirmed. He told us we were very lucky, all the roses in all the lights were faulty. If I hadn't made such a fuss about the smell, we could have all died in a house fire.

Maybe Kevin was protecting us.

8
DISMISSED AS AN ANXIOUS MOTHER

Just after Christmas 1982 a tabloid newspaper had a report on some research results from the geneticists department in Cardiff, that was showing that a lack of folic acid, could cause neural tube defects, recommending supplements prior to conception. I took this report to my GP. He prescribed supplements for me, which I continued to take until three months into my next pregnancy.

Throughout the entire pregnancy with my third child, Stephen, I was terrified. I was constantly in and out of hospital, fearful that something was going to go wrong. But despite what I had been through with Kevin, I wasn't shown much sympathy. In my notes, it was written that I was 'an anxious mother'.

Stephen was born 16 months to the day after Kevin died, and despite my trepidation, the birth went smoothly. When Stephen was a few weeks old, Gareth was helping me with a nappy change when he stated, 'I like my brother', he paused for a few seconds and said "is he staying?" My response was, "oh I hope so!".

As far as my husband was concerned, our family was complete, so we were both taken by surprise when I found out I was pregnant with my daughter. In fact, I didn't even know I was pregnant until I was three months on and noticed I was getting a bit of a tummy. I had none of the sickness I had suffered with the boy's, in so many ways, it was the best pregnancy, but in others, it was the worst. My husband was in denial and became uncommunicative, just as he had been when Kevin died. So although I was physically well, my mental health suffered, and it was to be the beginning of the end of our relationship.

My husband was on night shift when I went into labour so when I phoned him to say I needed to go into hospital, he was not impressed.

Once he had taken me into hospital, he asked the midwife "is she going to be long?" so instead of staying with me, he went back to work, leaving me alone, arriving back at the hospital with just minutes to spare before our daughter was born. To my horror, she was born with the umbilical cord wrapped around her neck twice, so her face was purple, her body was blue and her little legs were white. Thankfully the midwife managed to cut the cord in time so no lasting damage was done.

Ironically, my husband had always wanted a little girl and his disinterest quickly turned to joy. To this day, she is still 'daddy's girl'.

9
KEVIN'S LEGACY

When people ask me how many children I have, I say '3 surviving'. I can't just blank out Kevin's existence; He was part of me for nine months, and even now 40 years later, I still grieve for him.

After I left school I considered a nursing career but didn't think I was academic enough. In any case, I had my appendix out at the age of 17 and was the world's worst patient. Not only was I terrified of the whole procedure but I had a bad reaction to the anaesthetic and was violently sick. I married at 20 years old and I was 22 when I felt I had matured sufficiently to reconsider nursing and even went for an interview, but then I discovered I was pregnant with Gareth, so the idea was shelved once more and I did a variety of jobs - from stock control clerk to lifeguard.

But none of them gave me much satisfaction and after Kevin's death, I felt more and more about devoting myself to a career where I could help others. In 1989 I successfully applied to undertake nurse training. I started in October 1990 with 3 children under 9, so it wasn't easy. I qualified in March 1994. That same year saw the trial of Beverly Allitt - 'The Angel of Death' - the notorious serial killer convicted of murdering four children, attempting to murder three more and causing actual bodily harm to a further 6, while working as a nurse in the children's ward, so not only were permanent jobs hard to find, but the vetting processes had never been more rigorous. After six weeks of working on a gynaecological ward, I eventually got a job on the Special Care Baby Unit (now called Neonatal Intensive Care Unit), where I worked for 28 years until my retirement in 2022. At one time, I did consider training as a midwife but decided I couldn't cope with the responsibility; mistakes do happen I and could never forgive myself if I felt I had contributed to the loss of a baby.

Despite all my training, there were some instances when I found it difficult to care for babies with certain problems. I felt very traumatised in certain situations, and felt I couldn't give the care I should be able to give as I felt to emotionally involved. In those situations I asked to care for another patient instead. My work colleagues were very understanding in this situation, and it happened only on 1 or 2 occasions.

While 98% of births are straight forward, or relatively so, we still see dreadful tragedies, sometimes caused by the lack of training, shortage of skilful staff and sometimes a blasé approach of medical professionals. I've seen fractured skulls caused by clumsy forceps deliveries and even a layer of skin peeled from a baby's head with a suction cup. Every time such an incident occurs, it evokes the trauma of Kevin's birth, and brings back the sense of anger I felt at being treated as just a stupid mother who knew nothing.

Thankfully, both procedures and attitudes have changed dramatically over the years and had Kevin been born today, he might have survived, if only for a short time. I certainly would not have had my son whipped away from me without the opportunity to say a proper goodbye.

Nowadays, stillbirths, (more recently known as babies born sleeping), or babies who die soon after birth are placed in a cold cot to allow parents to spend time with them before they given a dignified funeral.

When Kevin died, babies were buried in a common grave containing 15 little bodies in three layers of five. As there were so many, they couldn't have been in coffins. I have spoken to so many parents who've experienced neonatal deaths, who don't even know where their babies are. And not long after I lost Kevin, the broadcaster and campaigner Esther Rantzen highlighted the issue in a TV programme about 'lost babies', whose parents were tormented by grief throughout their lives because they didn't know where they were. Today though, the babies are buried in tiny white coffins and their graves adorned with rose trees, windmills and toys in recognition of the lives they were denied or they are given the option of cremation.

In January 2018, a memorial garden was opened at the Hospital where Kevin was born, in conjunction with SANDS, a stillborn and neonatal death charity which didn't even exist at the time of Kevin's birth. There was absolutely no support back then, and indeed, it was six weeks before I discovered the existence of the Spina Bifida and Hydrocephalus Association, who were very helpful.

In many ways, I believe my experience made me a better person, personally and professionally. It's easy for someone to say 'Oh I know what you're going through', but actually they have no idea, unless they've experienced the same heartache themselves. Kevin's death has made me more empathic; more sensitive to other people's feelings.

My experience also taught me lessons about how to respond when parents suffer such a heart breaking loss. Please don't cross the road to avoid having to talk to someone who's lost their baby; Please speak to them or write to them, don't just pretend it never happened. I took great comfort in the weeks that followed Kevin's death from the fact that most people showed me kindness. The first few weeks saw my living room resemble a florist shop; I had lots of visitors and my son had so many toys bought for him. I had letters and cards not just from friends and family but also from people I hadn't seen in years. I've kept every card and letter I keep them safe and will treasure them always just as I treasure the memory of Kevin, my handsome boy.

I now have a stillbirth certificate which is written proof that he did exist. I didn't know until relatively   recently that one was available. I now have it, kept with all my cards and letters received at that time in my "Memorial   Tin".

10
LIFE GOES ON

Despite my grief, life with 3 growing children continued. We were a busy household. Both the boys enjoyed sport in school. They excelled in swimming, winning Welsh Age group titles as teenagers, and representing Wales on many occasions. They also qualified for the UK swimming championships. People do not realise how expensive supporting your child in sports is, and although talented, sponsorships were few and far between, so unfortunately they had to stop as the finances ran out, they were disappointed, but there was nothing I could do.

Gareth has always been a support when Stephen and Michelle were babies. I hadn't mentioned anything to Stephen about Kevin. I was going to tell him when he was older, when he was old enough to understand. I needn't have worried. When Stephen was almost 3, he saw me preparing some flowers to take to the cemetery. He said to me in his toddler way, "Pretty flowers mammy, they for Kevin?". I was gobsmacked! I asked him how he knew about Kevin? He told me that Gareth had told him he had another brother who went to live in heaven. He also told Michelle. Gareth is now married to Kerry Ann, and they have my beautiful grandaughter Skye, who has just started school. When Kerry went back to work one day of the week became "Nana day care day".

Stephen is my Rainbow Baby, he has always been caring and compassionate, but as a young adult he gave me many grey hairs. He did eventually settle down and is now married to Jess, and they have my gorgeous grandaughter Aria, who also spends the day with Nana once a week. They have just bought my childhood home from me, and are exited to be new home owners.

Michelle was also a talented swimmer, but her first love was ballet. At the age of 12, she had to choose between swimming and ballet. She chose ballet, and at 18 years old she moved to London to study dance and drama. I was a bit apprehensive of her going, but it was what she had always wanted to do.

24

In July 2005 she was caught up in the 7/7 bombings during her commute to college in Covent Garden. She travelled the Piccadilly line to college, normally with no problems, but this morning there were problems that made her late. Just shy of Holloway Road, the train came to an abrupt stop and there it stayed for serval hours. It was very hot and, due to the severe delays, very crowded. All the passengers were eventually taken back to Arsenal Station and allowed to alight. Just a few trains ahead, a suicide bomber detonated their device and it wasn't until they were above ground did they find out what happened. Two ladies who were on the train with Michelle took her under their wing, took her for a "cuppa" and they all went home in a taxi. I will be forever grateful to those ladies.

Meanwhile Rob and I were oblivious to what had happened as we had not had the radio or the TV on that morning; we were unaware of the tragedy in London. Mid-morning I had a call from my sister asking if Michelle was ok? After my response, she then explained what had happened in London. Thankfully I had only 20 minutes of panic before I had a text from her saying she was ok. I know that morning, both myself and my daughter were protected by, my son and her brother. Michelle managed to get home the next day, she was very shaken up and frightened. She talked about not wanting to go back to London. We talked a lot over the next few days and I told her I would support any decision she made, but she needed to think very deeply as this was something she had wanted to do since a young child. I told her that if she didn't go back, the terrorists had won! Don't let evil people ruin your dream.

Michelle returned to London to complete her diploma, and she never talked about that day again. The following year she met her husband Mike, they have two children, Lily is almost 15 and Frankie is 12, they brighten our lives. Michelle is now a Primary School Teacher and has settled in London. I will always be grateful to her in-laws for supporting and caring for her, as we lived so far away. Around 18 months ago Michelle and Mike separated, she is now a single mother and is thriving, with continued support from her in-laws.

For myself, life did change in 2000. My husband and I separated, and divorced in 2001. That was a difficult year. In 2002, I found a dating web site called "Match.com." I decided to fill in a profile, and was eventually contacted by a gentleman called Rob, who was recently divorced. We sent emails back and forth, and eventually met for the first time in February 2002. The rest is history! This year we have been together for 21 years. We married in 2005, we are very happy. I eventually told him about Kevin, and he read my account, as I had already been encouraged to write about my experience. After he had read my account, he hugged me. He suggested I publish this account, as he felt it would help people to understand why I still grieve. He has been very supportive and caring towards me, especially when Kevin's' birthday comes around. He took the first step to completing this project.

Attitudes and times have changed, but I have still come across people who cannot understand why I still talk about him. Many years ago, one particular work colleague, felt that I must be mentally ill as I still talked about him, especially around his birthday. I was quite shocked, thinking that they might be right?

I asked my GP for a referral to the mental health team and I was given an appointment to see a community Mental Health Nurse. I was with her for an hour, and I talked from my heart. She told me that I was not mentally ill, I was still grieving, and because of the traumatic experience I probably always would. She also told me not to take any notice of any comments made by people who couldn't possibly begin to understand.

Several years ago, a friend offered me the opportunity to visit a medium with her. I had thought about it on many an occasion, but had never been brave enough to go. I always thought if I arranged it, I would back out at the last minute. This is what had happened to my friend, she was going with her niece, but she had backed out. The appointment was for that evening, I spoke to Rob and he said it was up to me. I didn't really have time to think about it, so I said yes. My friend picked me up and we went to her house. When we arrived, my friend gave her name, and said I had come in place of her niece. The medium told me that I was meant to be there that night.

She spoke to me describing people and giving me names. Then she described a gentleman who had been standing back, but had now come forward. She gave my fathers shortened name, as he was always called. It wasn't a common name. She did tell me things no one else would have known. She then asked me if there was anyone specific I wanted to contact, I responded with a yes. At this point she said there was a young man with her. She started to describe him, and I had to stop her and tell her that I didn't know what he looked like. She then asked me how long he had lived for, and I told her he didn't. She said babies and children continue to grow in the spirit world. She then went on to tell me that ' there are some spirits who only need to experience life in the womb. These spirits are very special and will develop to have a very special role. These babies go on to become Angels, so technically you have given birth to an Angel. It might have been a load of rubbish, but it made me feel special, and so much better that my experience was not in vain. Every year on Kevin's birthday, my children send me flowers. I too, take flowers to Kevin's grave, that is all I can do

HE DID exist! I am the mother of 4 not 3!

Printed in Great Britain
by Amazon

As I held my new born son in my arms, I stroked his face, touched his lips, kissed his forehead and cried so much that my tears made his little face wet.

I thought if I cried long and hard enough, he would open his eyes and recognise me as his mum. He had a beautiful face that reminded me of my dad, and I dearly wanted to hold his hand and see his little body, which was swaddled in green theatre sheets.

But as I started to unwrap my precious little bundle, I was stopped by the midwife. She told me it was best that I didn't see him, and that was the last time I did.

I must have dozed off to sleep with him in my arms, but when I woke up, my baby was gone.

I had really wanted to see him. I wanted to understand why my baby had died. He had looked so normal, but the green sheets had masked deformities that, had he been born today, might have briefly survived.

At that time, we weren't officially allowed to name our little boy as his had been a stillbirth, but we wanted to call him Kevin. A few weeks later, I looked up the meaning of the name, which was 'handsome'. He was indeed handsome, and now, as it has been 40 years since his birth, I'm sure he would be handsome still.

ISBN 9798860994928

9 0

9 798860 994928